A
Change
is
Coming

A Change is Coming

BY HECTOR SOSA JR.

spring creek
BOOK COMPANY

Provo, Utah

ISBN 13: 978-0-9960974-2-0
e. 1

Published by:
Spring Creek Book Company
P.O. Box 50355
Provo, Utah 84605-0355

www.springcreekbooks.com

Cover design © Spring Creek Book Company

Printed in the United States of America
Printed on acid-free paper

TABLE OF CONTENTS

ACKNOWLEDGMENTS

I will use Lehi's words: "I know that I am a visionary man; for if I had not seen the things of God in a vision I should not have known the goodness of God." I want to acknowledge the men of God who have seen visions before me. They have shown that God continues to talk to his children through the ages.

I hope that Joel's prophecy continues to bless the people of this Earth: "And it shall come to pass afterward, that I will pour out my spirit upon all flesh; and your sons and your daughters shall prophesy, your old men shall dream dreams, your young men shall see visions: And also upon the servants and upon the handmaids in those days will I pour out my spirit."

I want to thank my wife Tammy. She has been truly a helpmeet for me. She has been gracious and very supportive through the process of writing this book. Without her, I would not be the man that I am today. I want to acknowledge my children, all seven of them: Cora, Lisa, Miranda, Gina, Patty, Jacob, and Heather. They have blessed my life and helped me to understand more of Heavenly Father's nature.

I want to acknowledge Bob Walker, a member of the Mormon Tabernacle Choir. He has been there whenever I needed somebody to talk to, and to exchange ideas and feelings about the last days.

Lastly, I want to acknowledge Chad Daybell. This book would not have come to light without his perseverance and dedication.

FOREWORD

BY TAMMY SOSA

While growing up as a member of The Church of Jesus Christ of Latter-day Saints, I often thought about what the last days would be like. I wondered if I would still be alive, and if so, how old would I be? Would I be married and have children? How bad would things get?

I don't think many of us can truly imagine what things will be like as the world gets worse. The best we can do is pray to know how we can prepare ourselves and our families. We need to strengthen our testimonies of Jesus Christ and follow His prophet here on earth.

It is an interesting experience to be married to Hector, who can see visions of what is to come. It is also a great blessing, and it has allowed us to become prepared for the trials and troubles that are coming soon.

While the visions in this book pertain to our family, it is my hope that it will inspire others to prepare themselves for the calamities that will come before the Second Coming of Jesus Christ. For those who are already preparing, may it strengthen your resolve and show that you are not alone.

Prophets have testified of these times since the beginning. It is our privilege to live through them.

Tammy Sosa
April 2015

CHAPTER ONE

AN INHERITED GIFT

My name is Hector Sosa. I was born in Puerto Rico, and I have the not-always-welcome gift of seeing future events in dreams. I also sometimes see these events in waking visions. This is a gift that is fairly common among people of my heritage, and in my case I have inherited this trait from my mother.

The visions I see are always an answer to a specific question I have asked the Lord. I don't always receive the answer immediately, but when I do, it is often quite memorable. My wonderful wife Tammy has been awakened many nights to find me in the midst of a dream. She has patiently listened as I wake up and then describe what I have seen.

When I have a waking vision, I often see future events superimposed over the actual locations. For example, I might be driving along and suddenly see bricks falling off buildings on the side of the road as if an earthquake is happening. Or I might see cracks developing in the road ahead. It is a little unsettling for me, but I have gotten used to it.

Another factor about my dreams is that the answers I receive through them pertain only to the lives of my family members. The dreams and visions are intended for my own benefit and growth, or to guide me as I assist or warn my relatives.

Since these dreams and visions apply only to my family, the scenarios I have seen mainly take place in central Utah or near Puerto Rico and the southeast coast of the United States. I am sharing them publicly, however, in the hopes that others can take what I have learned and apply it in their own lives. The scenarios I describe in this book might not directly impact you, but there is a good chance that you will be impacted in a similar way in the coming years.

I want to emphasize that I do not have stewardship over anyone outside my family, and especially not other members of the Church of Jesus Christ of Latter-day Saints. I fully support the LDS Church's First Presidency, Quorum of the Twelve Apostles, and all other church leaders, and I will follow their counsel as these future events unfold.

I realize that many of the events I describe are frightening, but I feel my overall message is one of hope. The Lord will provide a way for his faithful Saints to be preserved and even prosper in the coming years.

Life in Puerto Rico

As I mentioned, I was born on the island of Puerto Rico, and that is where I spent my childhood. My family lived in a small town. Our home was a simple concrete house with slick floor tiles. We didn't have rugs or carpet, because it was so humid on the island that such things would quickly get moldy.

My family wasn't rich, but we were much better off than most people on the island. My father was a Master

Sergeant in the U.S. Air National Guard. He was a medical technician and supervised one of the labs at the local base. My mother managed the household and took care of the children. I am the oldest child, and I have a brother and a sister.

When I was in fourth grade, my parents decided it was time to move out into the country. They arranged to have a redwood Swiss chalet imported from Washington state for our family to live in. The various parts of the house were delivered to a one-acre property we owned outside of town, and my family assembled it there and added a solar heater system on the roof. Such a house was a unique sight in Puerto Rico.

I was happy to live in the country. My father would go stateside for his two-week National Guard drills in Savannah, Georgia, and he would come back with pheasants, bobwhite quail, and peacocks. These birds were added to our collection of animals, which included egg-laying chickens, ducks, geese, goats, and the occasional horse.

We could see Puerto Rico's northern coast from our porch. I had a telescope, and as I looked through it toward the ocean I could see oil tankers passing by. I could read the words on the sides of the ships, such as Shell or Exxon. I sometimes even saw huge container ships.

As with many Puerto Ricans, I have Taino blood coursing through my veins. The Tainos come from the Arawak branch of Native Americans, who were the indigenous peoples of the Caribbean islands.

I strongly identify with the Taino culture. Our house was near El Yunque mountain, which the Tainos refer to as the throne of Yukiyu, the god of goodness and agriculture. He protected the Taino people from his mountain throne.

The mountain is one of the tallest peaks in Puerto Rico, and it nearly always is shrouded in a mist. The area receives more than 100 inches of rain each year, and I essentially lived in a rainforest. All of that rain made our vegetable gardens flourish. We also had many exotic tropical fruit trees, including mango trees where the fruit grew to the size of pineapples.

It was quite a chore, though, to keep the jungle under control. We would go out together and use six-foot long machetes to clear several acres of jungle a week. My father owned a big green truck, which was our primary mode of transportation for such projects.

One of the biggest challenges was keeping the native grasses at bay. The pampa grass had razor sharp edges and could grow an inch a day. We had to constantly keep things cut down.

My Family Heritage

Puerto Rico actually consists of several islands. There is the main island, and then other much smaller ones, such as Vieques, Culebra, and Mona. My mother was raised on Vieques. She lived there with her grandfather, who was a tough old rancher.

The U.S. Navy used most of Vieques for target practice, and residents would actually get injured. The

This is El Yunque mountain. This is the view I saw every time I stepped into our backyard growing up in Puerto Rico.

This image is the Sol of Jayuya. It is one of the many symbols on the ceremonial Taino grounds that were used by my ancestors for playing something akin to soccer. I've always associated this symbol with Yukiyu.

Navy would bring in their aircraft carriers, the pilots would become certified by making bombing runs at the island. Puerto Ricans finally took a stand after a civilian security guard was accidentally killed, and the bombing stopped.

Anyway, my mother grew up there. She is descended from Mandinka slaves, who were brought to Puerto Rico from the Ivory Coast in West Africa. She is still really old-fashioned from growing up on Vieques. Their main mode of transportation was horse-drawn carriages even into the 1950s. There was no technology. She relied on tools such as a sewing machine with foot pedals.

On my father's side I am descended from the Castillian people of Spain. I am a distant cousin of baseball star Sammy Sosa. As I mentioned, I am also a descendant of the Arawak tribe from the Brazilian jungles. So I am quite a mix of nationalities from all over the world.

I went on an LDS mission to Barcelona, Spain, where I learned the Catalonian language. I also understand French and Portuguese. When I was on my mission, most everyone thought I was a rich Arab. People would approach me and ask, "Why are you hanging out with these American kids?"

Raised in the Catholic Faith

I haven't always been a Latter-day Saint. My parents raised me in the Catholic faith. One of the Catholic prayers is called "Our Father." It is a humble supplication to God that we would say on the island.

I offer the following prayer in Taino…
Guakia Baba Turey toca Guami-ke-ni
Guarico guakia Tayno-ti Bo-matum;
Busica guakia Para yucubia Aje-cazabi;
Juracan-jua Maboya-jua Yukiyu-Jan;
Dio-sa Nabori daca Jan Jan Catu

The English equivalent is:
Our Father is in the sky,
Lord of land and water, Lord of moon and sun,
Come to us, good and tall, big and generous,
Give to us rain plants and yams bread;
Bad spirit, no, ghost, no, good spirit, yes;
of God, servant am I, so be it.

Hurricane David

In August of 1979, Hurricane David approached Puerto Rico, and we stayed with my father's parents to ride out the storm.

It is good that we left, because the hurricane smashed our house. It lifted the solar panels and smashed them into one side of the gabled roof. That whole side of the roof came down. My father found it on the ground when he checked on the house.

He and a brother-in-law nailed the roof back on as best as they could. As you can imagine, there were a lot of leaks. We ended up having to use several pots and pans to catch the water whenever it rained. We ended up removing all of the bloated corkboard and linoleum throughout the house.

The water barrel for the solar heater system had smashed the other side of the house, so the kitchen had an enormous dent in it. The wood rotted, and it turned into a hole that had some linoleum barely covering it.

In the end, the house was condemned, and the storm essentially cost us everything. Many items we owned were repossessed. It was a challenging time for us.

A Golden Family

As I mentioned, we were Catholic for many years. Then we literally stumbled into sister missionaries from the LDS Church soon after the hurricane. My mother had an impression that she needed to be at the recently opened Plaza Caroline Mall at 7 p.m.

While at the mall, she ran into these sister missionaries from the Church. They talked for a few minutes, and they got our family's information. Soon after my mother finally arrived home from the mall at around 9 p.m., Elder Michael Shake and Elder Pedro Guerrero knocked on our door.

My parents were quite surprised, since our house was in the countryside and people routinely got lost on the way. My parents welcomed their message, and we joined the LDS Church on February 17, 1980 when I was 13 years old.

Most of my family members were baptized that same day. We were one of those "Golden Families." Of course, trials started as soon as we were baptized.

While we were living in the broken house, my father contracted liver flukes when he was away at his annual

Air National Guard training in Louisiana. He was in a hospital near our home for more than a year. There were several times we went to the hospital expecting it to be my father's last day on earth.

We had many miracles happen during this time. The most memorable one was when my mother drove our Honda Civic to the hospital. This particular time we did not have enough gas money to make it there. My mother offered a prayer, then she got in the car and drove to see my father. The gas never ran out.

I received a lot of my faith in God from her, just like Helaman's 2,000 stripling warriors in the Book of Mormon did from their mothers.

At long last my father was able to return home. He received a large compensation check after surviving his ordeal in the hospital. My parents decided to use that money to leave Puerto Rico for Utah.

This was my first school picture at Enterprise High. It was taken shortly after we got there on August of 1982. That T-shirt was bought on the island a few weeks before.

CHAPTER TWO

SETTLING IN UTAH

It was 1982 when we bought some duffel bags and clothes from the local Sears store and left our island home. We flew from San Juan to Dallas, then we took a Greyhound bus from there to Salt Lake City.

My parents bought a beat-up station wagon in Salt Lake, which we then traveled in south toward St. George, Utah, visiting several returned missionaries along the way that we had known in Puerto Rico.

We arrived in St. George in late July 1982. The temperature was hovering around 100 degrees, and it felt like everything was on fire. The weather was way too hot for my mother. She couldn't imagine living there for very long.

My parents remembered a missionary that was from the nearby town of Enterprise, and we traveled there a couple of weeks later.

My parents liked the town, so we settled there and I enrolled at Enterprise High School. I'll never forget the tour I was given of the school. I was stunned when I saw that they played basketball on an indoor wooden court. In Puerto Rico, only professional basketball players were allowed to play on that kind of court. Everybody else had to play on concrete courts.

I graduated from Enterprise High School in 1985. My parents soon moved to Kanab, Utah for about a year while I attended Dixie College in St. George.

We then moved to Mesa, Arizona and were part of the Lehi Stake. At that point I served my LDS mission in Barcelona, Spain from 1987 to 1989, and when I returned home my parents had moved once again, this time to Wilcox, Arizona.

One of my final missionary companions, Ryan Jarvis, was from Pima, Arizona. He convinced me to attend Eastern Arizona College, and I earned my Associates of Applied Science Degree as a Computer Information Specialist in December 1994.

That is where I met my first wife, Cindylou Martin. We were married in the summer of 1995. A year later our fraternal twins, Patricia and Jacob, were born. Unfortunately, the marriage did not last long and we were divorced by 1999.

I am now married to the former Tammy Gustafson, who grew up in Highland, Utah and served in the Missouri Independence Mission. We were married in the Timpanogos Temple on December 15, 2000.

This is the second marriage for both of us and we share six girls and one boy, including two sets of twins. All of them but one have now graduated from high school.

I am currently a Database Engineer and have worked with computers for more than two decades. I run several websites myself, including four web forums. I was working with computers before there was the commercial Internet. It has really been interesting to watch how technology has helped spread the Gospel of

Jesus Christ across the world, and also in our personal lives. I really love having my phone read the scriptures aloud to me.

Allergic to Modern Life

About a decade ago, I developed a severe reaction to anything that contained petroleum. I also developed intolerances to lactose and wheat. I also became allergic to wool and cedar.

When these allergies started, I would be sick for days if I smelled hand lotions, nail polish, any kind of carpenter or carpet glues, colognes, perfumes, or a number of other things. I wasn't able to be in public places for a number of years. I had to wear a face mask with a carbon liner to even set foot in a church building.

The allergies have subsided a little recently. I can last about 15 minutes now before I start feeling ill. I can usually stay until I take the sacrament, but I have to leave soon afterward.

About a year ago, I was finally able to go to malls and movie theaters. I'm fine when I'm outside. Pollen, hay, and dust don't bother me. So basically, I'm allergic to modern civilization!

It is frustrating, because it seems like there should be a solution. I have sought help from basically every avenue. My father ran a sample lab for a hospital for 11 years, and my wife is a biomedical technician at a local hospital, but we're still not sure what is causing it.

I'm very familiar with Nambudripad's Allergy Elimination Techniques (NAET). It just hasn't worked

I rely on a mask to help me through many indoor situations.
I have allergies to petroleum-based products. I'm essentially
allergic to modern life!

for me, because my illness is composed of several layered afflictions that have both environmental and genetic components.

I've been able to control the environmental stuff, but not the genetic components. Both of my parents and siblings have similar symptoms. But I make the best of it!

CHAPTER THREE

VISIONS AS A YOUNG MAN

I started having dreams and visions when I was around ten years old in Puerto Rico, which was three years before I joined the LDS Church. The majority of my visions and dreams have been about my future.

I didn't understand what these various dreams meant until recently. The dreams that have come true so far were essentially promptings commanding me to do certain things, and I have seen those fulfilled if I did what I was shown. I have also had a few face-to-face visitations from spiritual beings.

As a young boy, I would often look at the cloud-covered peak of El Yunque mountain where the gods supposedly lived. I always tried to imagine what Yukiyu looked like. He is one of the supreme deities in Taino lore, and I just wanted a better picture in my mind of him.

One Saturday morning after finishing my chores, I went to gaze at El Yunque again. To my great surprise, I saw the heavens open to the side as a curtain would, and I clearly saw a bearded man sitting on a throne. This man had lighter skin than I had, and he was wearing a white robe with a tan over-robe. His arms were gently resting on the armrests of the throne. The throne was a simple affair. I sensed it was made to give precedence to the person who sat in it.

I believed that this was Yukiyu. He looked in my direction, then the heavens closed like a curtain again. This was the first vision I remember.

Hill with a Red Moon

I then had a dream repeated over several nights with a large red moon featured prominently. I was in a field with many people and the land was flat. The land had patches of green and bare dirt. To my right was a range of mountains. Directly in front of me was a hill and the red moon shone directly behind it.

There was a path carved on the face of the hill that I could see. It appeared that the path curved back and forth three times before it got to the top.

At the top of the hill I noticed some sort of contraption that shone brightly. It stood on the left side of the hill. There were people dressed in white robes at the top of the hill and they conveyed people to the contraption. To my child eyes, the contraption looked like the chariot of fire that took Elijah.

Maybe it is a symbolic dream, but I feel this event might still be fulfilled in the coming years.

Ocean Complaining

Another dream I had was about the ocean. I was standing at night, with a full moon, on a road that had a guardrail. On the other side of the guardrail was a beach. I could hear the surf breaking against the sand and rocks. It was swishing back and forth. The water then started swishing harder and harder as if the ocean was angry. The water receded back into the ocean. I then heard a very angry feminine voice. The earth itself was crying out in frustration.

"They have polluted me," the earth said. "They have contaminated me. I am in constant pain. The Creator has forbidden me to cleanse myself again with water. I wait for the time when my righteous anger will be released. I will cleanse myself of this pollution. I will rid myself of the wicked sons of man. They are wicked as the sons of Adam of old."

Sharing My Mother's Gift

As I mentioned, these types of dreams weren't unusual in my culture. We understood that such messages were meant to assist us in some way. Their meanings weren't always clear, but we also knew they weren't accidental or without purpose.

My mother and I often had the same dreams, and we would discuss them. When we moved to Enterprise, she shared a dream she'd had where people were driving a truck loaded with supplies up a mountain road. As they reached a camp, a veil or curtain came down behind them to hide the camp so that it couldn't be seen by outsiders. I will discuss this dream later in the book in its proper sequence, but because of dreams like this, she wondered about what was coming in the future.

Through a fellow church member, she found out about a book entitled *Prophecy: Key to the Future* by Duane S. Crowther. The book is a wonderful summary of the prophecies given by LDS Church leaders over the years, along with scriptural passages to support them.

This book really opened my mother's eyes to the fact that other Church members had also seen many of the events she had seen in dreams. She also realized that the scriptures were filled with similar dreams given to people throughout the centuries.

My mother gave me a copy of that book, and I studied it thoroughly. It helped us both gain a better understanding of what we were being shown.

A Time Without Dreams

As I grew older and got busy with college, marriage, and children, I had a period where I did not have dreams. These were years of suffering, mostly by my own doing. My turning point came when I was in the local mall with my wife, Tammy. We stopped at Jon McNaughton's store. One painting caught my eye. I was in awe and very still. I felt the Spirit testify of Jesus Christ and that he was soon to come again.

This painting now hangs on my dining room wall.

A Life-Changing Dream

Not long after the experience at the mall, I had a life-changing dream in May 2009.

In the dream, I was in a living room. I looked around and it seemed like some sort of party was going on. There were quite a few people mingling around the house. It was one of those open floor plans. The living room, kitchen, and dining room were visible from anywhere in the house. After a while, I noticed someone who

A Sosa family photo with my parents and siblings.

A photo of me with our painting "Peace is Coming" by Jon McNaughton.

appeared to be the matron of the house. She was wearing a long, red, cotton dress. She was moving around among the guests.

I noticed one guest who seemed out of place. He was wearing jeans and an old, beat-up, green army coat. He had longish hair and a neatly trimmed beard. The matron stopped and talked with him a few times.

By now, I was wondering why I was there. While I was pondering my thoughts, a few people brought a low rectangular wooden table into the living room. Then another person brought one of those green plastic containers you can buy at Wal-Mart.

I came closer to see what was happening. I noticed the matron and the bearded man were now together discussing something.

I was standing near one end of the green container. The matron and the man walked up to the other side of it, and I heard the matron tell him they had run out of wine.

I asked myself, "I don't drink wine, so why is wine here?"

I looked into the container and noticed that it was filled about half-way with water. While I was looking inside the container, the man put his hand inside with his palm facing away from me. He then moved his hand away from me, stirring the water and creating a small wake. As the wake subsided, the water started turning into wine.

I was extremely surprised when I saw that. My eyes immediately searched the face of the man, and I looked into his eyes. At that moment, I knew it was Jesus Christ.

My eyes filled with tears. I looked down for a couple seconds to clear my eyes, then I looked back up into his eyes. He looked at me for a moment and in a soft voice said, "Everything will be all right."

That's when I woke up and told my wife Tammy about it. I believe that was the moment where my life changed for the best.

These dreams and visions have become much more frequent since 2014. I've been having an increasing sense of impending doom concerning our country. I've been waking up screaming, crying, and inspired—sometimes all three at the same time. This has caused some scary moments for my wife and children.

Despite the sense of doom, I also feel I am being prepared to serve how and where the Lord needs me. As you read further into the book, you'll see I feel that my wife and I will be assigned to help others reach safety when times get tough.

I want to re-emphasize that I only have stewardship over my family. I do not claim to tell the Church or anyone else what to do. I have no desire to lead in any capacity. I'm just another voice of warning, and I'm sharing what I've been given in the hope others will make wise preparations for the days ahead.

I fully support my Church leaders. I know they are inspired men. For example, one recent night my Stake President and his counselors knocked on our front door. I invited them in, and I called the whole family down to hear what they had to say.

Their message was simple yet powerful. They exhorted us to have prayer as a family in the morning and at night. We have heeded that counsel. My family and I have increased the amount of prayers we are doing. My wife and I are praying on our knees every night. We have family prayers early in the morning and before going to bed.

We have noticed that a different spirit has taken residence in our home. There is a pleasant feeling there. We know that the Lord sent our stake leaders to us that night to help us stay on the right path.

CHAPTER FOUR

The First Earthquake

On Wednesday evening, August 21, 2014, I was in bed talking to my wife. Then suddenly I felt like my head was violently shaking. It was very confusing. The roof of my top palate and my sinuses felt like I was driving fast over railroad ties. Then I started hearing things falling to the ground and breaking.

I asked my wife, "Is the house shaking?"

"No," she said. "Why?"

"I feel like I'm in the middle of an earthquake."

This sensation lasted around eight minutes. When it ended, I was feeling very nauseous and shaken up. I walked to the kitchen to take medication for my headache. I got back in bed and had a very strong urge to put our vases on the floor and take the paintings off the walls.

I was sure this was a warning, so we packed the vases and took down the paintings and pictures. Our two TVs were placed face down on the carpet.

I was so shaken up by this that we made plans to eat dinner with my in-laws and let them know about my experience. We met them for dinner at a local restaurant. I told them about the dream and how I felt we needed to be prepared.

To my immense relief, we found that they were ready with 72-hour kits, along with food and water storage.

Brick Buildings Fall

So why did I have this vivid shaking experience? Well, it woke me up both physically and spiritually. It is my understanding that there will be two noteworthy earthquakes in Utah in the near future.

The first one that will strike is not the Big One that everyone fears, but it will cause enough significant damage to suspend services for a couple of weeks in some parts of Utah.

I was shown that in the first earthquake, older buildings made of brick will shift and have significant damage, and any structure built out of cinder blocks without rebar will likely come down.

I didn't see a whole lot of damage in my own Springville neighborhood. Most of the homes there are fairly new, and they held up well. However, the earthquake happened before sunrise, and it knocked the electricity out. I saw Tammy and I leaving our home and checking on our neighbors early in the morning as the sun started to creep over the mountain to the east.

This dream was so strong that I kept seeing superimposed images on buildings and landscapes for about two weeks after I had it. The most vivid images came during a trip we took to the Cabela's store in Lehi. In that area I viewed superimposed images of the damaged buildings, and I saw cracks in the road.

On the way back home, we got off I-15 and drove east on Center Street in Provo. I saw that pretty much all of the brick buildings on Center Street were damaged, with piles of bricks everywhere on the sidewalks and into the street. Nearly every cinderblock building we passed had partially collapsed.

I had a vision showing newspaper articles about the quake. The headlines were all similar, such as "The Big One Came. We Survived."

All of the city and state crews got right to work taking care of the problems. About two weeks after the earthquake, much of the major cleanup was completed. Numerous buildings were condemned and cordoned off, and some were simply being demolished because they were unsafe to enter.

Most of the streets were repaired to the point they were at least drivable.

The reactions by the citizens living along Utah's Wasatch Front was mixed. For some, it was a wake-up call. After watching disasters happen all around the globe for decades, they finally realized something catastrophic could actually happen in Utah.

However, for others it was almost a time to celebrate. It was like they were saying, "Hurray! The Big One has come. Now we can quit worrying about such things and get back to living our lives."

A Learning Experience

As these premonitions and visions kept coming, I felt a voice in my head saying, "You will see a sign two days before it happens."

I had no idea what I was supposed to be looking for, but I felt that the earthquake would happen sometime in October 2014.

The first earthquake in Utah will cause substantial damage.
Portions of brick buildings will tumble into the streets.

I was fully prepared and expecting it to strike. So I was somewhat baffled when the earthquake did not come during that month. At first I was rather angry it hadn't happened, mostly because of my pride. The irony is that I have been asking the Lord to keep pride away from my heart, and yet I still fell prey to it in this instance. It was quite embarrassing to say the least.

The voice of the Lord came to me and explained, "I did not give you dates. You took it upon yourself to put dates on this particular vision. Do not give dates. Please do not be so hard on yourself. As you already know, you are your own harshest critic. You have already tortured yourself enough to pay for your arrogance several times over. Let it go."

Then a few hours later I felt the Lord's voice again. "I have heard the prayers of the righteous," he said. "I have stayed my hand."

So I asked, "When will it happen?"

The answer I was given was "Soon."

So the lesson I learned is that I should not put dates on the events I see in dreams. But I do sense that whenever it is going to happen, it's imminent. I know that the Lord keeps time differently, so I'm not giving time frames. I do know that we will have a sign of some sort about two days before the event happens.

As far as I know, the sign won't be given just to me. It will be a very public thing that could be dismissed if we are not looking for it. I actually don't know what it will be. I have asked for clarification but I haven't been told more.

The sense I get is that it will be a matter of faith. If we are listening to the Spirit, we will recognize the sign. Until then, peace be unto your heart. Let your mind be not troubled, for the Lord will take care of us.

Roads and freeways will be damaged during the first earthquake, but repairs will be made within a few weeks.

CHAPTER FIVE

Plagues and Sicknesses

I always wondered about the plagues spoken of that will be part of the judgments of God poured upon the world. I know that there are going to be at least two major outbreaks.

I was recently watching a *Star Trek: Deep Space Nine* episode called "The Quickening." (It is season 4, episode 23 for all you Trekkies.) In the episode, the population of a planet has been infected with a plague that gives them purple lesions.

As I watched the show, the Spirit whispered to me that this is what the first plague will look like. A few days later one of my cousins from Puerto Rico posted a picture of a Chikungunya rash. As soon as I saw it, the Spirit whispered that this is what the second plague will look like. Chikungunya is a little-known virus that is afflicting a lot of people in tropical regions.

First Plague with Purple Lesions

I have actually had a group of dreams dealing with the first plague with purple lesions. These dreams have been snippets that last 30 seconds or less.

I saw that no age group was safe from the disease. The most noticeable aspect of this plague was that at the later stages, the veiny lesions were dark purple. There was a central nub in the skin from where tentacle-like lesions

Here is an illustration of the first plague. The lesions will be purple and there will be a central nub in the skin from where the tentacle-like lesions will spread.

spread. These were quite noticeable on the top of the hands, cheeks, and forehead. The people who contracted it were very sickly and had a sheen of sweat across their bodies, as if they had a high fever.

I saw vistas of towns and cities where the plague had struck. I spent a lot of the dreams walking through the streets of Salt Lake City and other communities looking at people's front doors. Each door had a FEMA-type poster or sign that indicated how many people had died in the house.

Most houses had posters marked to show at least one death. I did notice a lot of black body bags on the front and back porches of the homes.

People were very afraid of this plague. It spread rapidly, and it also affected people quickly after they contracted it. After a while, when adult family members knew they were infected, they would put themselves in the body bags and zip them up to their chests to save their family members the trouble. Then they waited to die, since there was no cure. Some people died fairly quickly while others took a few days to die.

I was spared from seeing the part where their eyes basically melted from their faces. I only know this will happen from reading other accounts.

Second Plague with White Lesions

As I said earlier, this second plague starts out like a cold, very similar to the Chikungunya virus infection. People have fevers, shakes, and are in a lot of pain. The skin eventually breaks out in blisters. This plague

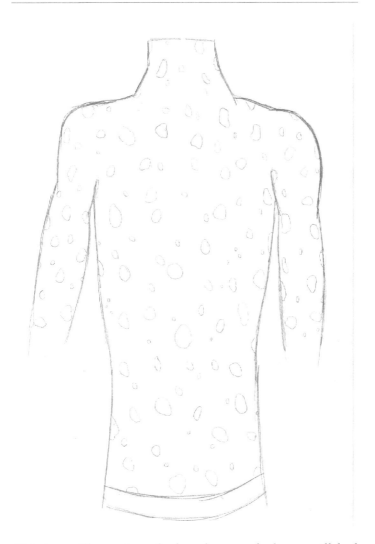

This is an illustration of what the second plague will look like. The most prominent feature is white lesions all over the body.

reminds me a lot of when I had chicken pox, only the blisters have a whiter and thicker pus.

People were in quite a bit of pain in the later stages. I didn't see much of this one, only what it looked like. I saw a middle aged man with his shirt off and I was mostly looking at his back, neck, and arms. Those body parts were covered in the thick white blisters, and I would suppose it covered his entire body.

I'm very visual and pictures help me visualize a lot of this latter-day stuff. So I described to my daughter what I saw, and she sketched my descriptions of the plagues.

I'm not saying that they will look exactly like this, but these drawings are very close to what I saw. I don't want people to freak out. I just want to make people aware that these plagues are coming.

CHAPTER SIX

THE GATHERING BEGINS

One aspect of the future I had seen but had rarely heard discussed was the idea of the Lord calling out his people in the latter days. I had been shown that the Church leaders would prepare places for the Saints to take refuge when troubles began across the world.

Then when the time was right, the prophet would work through priesthood channels to organize the stakes and have the people get to safety.

This concept is clear in the Book of Mormon. Several times throughout the book the Lord inspires his prophets to lead righteous groups to safety, including the very first story when Lehi leaves Jerusalem and goes into the wilderness.

Then I read two books by a woman named Julie Rowe. She had a near-death experience and was shown many of the same things I was. It hit me like a thunderbolt as she described what she called "The Gathering."

Julie's books helped clarify for me many of the dreams I'd been having concerning the future. I later learned that many people have had similar dreams concerning this event.

Before I go on, I want to make it clear that I don't speak for the LDS Church. I'm simply relaying what I've observed through the various instruments God uses to speak to me.

Concerning how this gathering begins (also referred to by some people as the call-out), we will know when it is transpiring if we are in tune with The Spirit. That's why the General Authorities have been admonishing us to set our houses in order, because this event will mark the opening acts for the judgments of God being poured out onto the wicked of the world.

Gathering in Waves

As I prayed for more information about this event, I was given several analogies for waves: a pebble in a pond, an onion being peeled layer by layer, the surf on a sea shore. I then saw orderly waves of people being called at different times throughout the coming months and years.

The very first ones were the people who were completely prepared. Some were asked by Church leaders to prepare certain areas and bring their supplies to the designated places. Meanwhile, others were guided by the Spirit to move to different locations where their talents and strengths would be best served.

Many of these people were prompted by the Spirit to move for their own protection. The Lord was directing them so they could avoid the dangers and disasters that will soon strike their cities.

To me it seemed like some sort of board game where the Lord was putting his pieces where they belonged before the game actually starts. These people will be in place to help the rest of the waves of people coming behind them.

I used to wonder when this part of the plan would start, but it is clear that these promptings and moves are now underway. The Lord is positioning his faithful Saints to be where they need to be. The average Church member might hear of a neighbor moving and not really understand why. They might even think it is a bad decision, but the Lord is behind these moves.

God is a God of order. The Saints who are watching for the signs will know something is happening. Sadly, the majority of the Saints will be unaware.

When the Church leadership calls the Saints to begin gathering, many will ignore the message and others will miss it entirely. If we are not in tune with the Spirit, the instructions will seem inconsequential, and people will turn back to their daily meanderings.

I do have a sense that the call out will start soon. Notice I didn't say it will fully happen, just that it will start. This initial gathering will be ongoing for several months. Individual families will take part as the timing is right for them. I see it as a call to complete our final preparations and to stand ready.

An Invitation to Leave

When those Saints are in position and deteriorating world conditions dictate, the Lord will initiate the next step in his plan. The prophet will invite the LDS Church members to leave their homes and gather into the places of refuge that have been prepared.

I was shown this vividly that it will be done on a stake level, rather than to the entire church. That is why different people see different scenarios, because every stake has its own circumstances and conditions. Some stakes, such as those in small towns or in mountainous regions, will actually stay where they are and serve as gathering places.

I was shown how things will happen in my stake in Springville. I was in a meeting after church at night. I wasn't wearing my allergy mask. We were in my stake center, and someone I didn't recognize was reading a letter from the First Presidency. He was likely an area authority. It definitely wasn't someone from my stake.

He told the congregation, "Brothers and sisters, the time has come. Heavenly Father is calling us out of Babylon. This has been prophesied for many years. The time is now."

Several people jumped up and said, "What do you mean 'The time is now'?"

The man put the letter down on the pulpit and said, "We have 48 hours to complete our preparations, then we need to leave."

His words caused a big commotion among the members. Some people said he was crazy, but some of us welcomed the announcement. We had been waiting for it, and it was a relief the time had come.

In a separate wide-awake vision related to this announcement, I saw a man coming up the sidewalk toward my home. He was in his early 60s and husky with wavy gray hair. He was very sure and confident. He felt familiar to me, and I will recognize him instantly when I see him.

The man was wearing a white suit and looked like a temple worker. He had been assigned several families to check on, and he was making sure these people had received the message.

He turned up our walkway and asked, "Brother Sosa, are you ready?"

"Yes, we are ready," I said. "We've been waiting for this."

He nodded and asked, "Do you need help with your preparations?"

"Yes, we do."

"Very well," he said. "I will send a couple of young men over here with a truck to help you."

Then the vision ended.

Follow the Counsel of the Church Leaders

There are dark forces and secret combinations watching the Church. They seek to bring it down. This has always been the case, but their power and efforts are growing. Many members of the Church will be misled and go down incorrect paths.

This is part of the reason the General Authorities have been counseling the members to get their lives in order and to be close to the Spirit.

While I've been a member of the church, announcements have been made through letters sent to stake presidents and bishops. These are then read at stake conferences and ward conferences. The same pattern will be followed for this announcement to gather. A very public announcement, such as during General

Conference, would make things more difficult for members. The stake level is where these kinds of matters are handled.

I recently had a vivid dream that emphasized this point. The dream started with me seated with my family at the usual bench in our chapel. I was looking up at the podium. My current stake president was at the podium reading a letter that was sent from the Brethren.

A personage in a white robe, sandals, a trimmed beard, and longish hair appeared out of thin air, facing the podium. The stake president had not noticed the new arrival. The personage walked toward the podium then stopped. At that point the stake president noticed him and immediately fell to his knees. The personage placed his right hand on the stake president's shoulder and pulled him to his feet.

By this time I had no doubt in my mind who this personage was. He faced the pews and walked down the steps toward me. He stopped right in front of me and gazed into my eyes. That's when I woke up.

I feel the dream was meant to show me that my stake president is known to the Lord, and that my stake president knows the Lord. John 10:27 reads, "My sheep hear my voice, and I know them, and they follow me."

When he walked to where I was seated simply means that he is coming and that I should pay attention to him first and to trust the words of my stake president.

An Organized Exodus

In another vision, I was standing in front of the

Church's distribution center near my home in west Springville. This was a day or two after the gathering announcement, and the place was very busy. There were hundreds of people there.

The concrete barriers were gone that usually blocked vehicles from getting near the building. Instead, there were white moving vans of various sizes getting loaded with supplies. It was early morning, but it wasn't really cold. The fields nearby were plowed but not planted, leading me to think this was late spring.

Yellow school buses were parked by the distribution center, as well as six other buses lined up at the nearby stake center. These buses seemed to be from local religious-based preparatory schools, rather than from the local school district.

I saw several pickup trucks in the parking lot of the stake center, but I didn't see many people there. Everyone seemed to be helping at the distribution center.

Meanwhile, cars zoomed by us on the road that passes east of Wal-Mart like nothing exciting was happening, I thought it was curious that people weren't questioning what was going on. We were purposely doing everything at a steady pace, though, to avoid attracting attention to ourselves.

The days of normalcy were growing short. Soon the faithful Saints would be gathered in the places of refuge, and those who stayed behind would need to fend for themselves.

My family and I are preparing and are ready to leave when we are asked to do so. My wife and I already decided that we are going to leave everything behind the minute there is even a hint of any sort of gathering or call out.

My kids are all on board with us on our emergency preparations. Thankfully they've taken everything we've told them about upcoming events in stride. I have one child who is living with my sister while attending college out of state. I have sent emergency supplies to them, and we have given them instructions on reuniting if that time comes.

CHAPTER SEVEN

DEPARTURE TO THE CAMPS

I was next shown that members of my stake departed from our stake center. Some rode in the yellow buses, and others traveled in the convoy of pickup trucks. It was very calm and organized, and our family members went with them. My wife and I stayed behind, with plans to join them later.

They crossed through Mapleton without much fanfare, and they noticed gatherings at other stake centers that they passed. Then they began the journey up Spanish Fork Canyon toward a camping area.

I have been shown the details of three different camps. I know there will be dozens of other camps in the Rocky Mountains, but these are the ones that pertain to my family.

At the time of the gathering, the Heber Valley Camp will have expanded a bit from its present size, and it will be very organized. The camp is in really good shape right now, but there will be additional improvements made between now and then.

Another location I have seen is Sanpete County, which includes several cities, beginning with Fairview on the north end and Manti to the south. This whole valley will be considered a place of refuge. The members who are already there will stay and assist those who come from the Wasatch Front and other areas.

The homes within the cities will serve as shelters for women and children, and thousands of tents will be placed for everyone else to live in. Many of the basic utilities and infrastructure will still function in many of the smaller towns. The Saints will find ways to generate their own power and maintain running water.

I know that there will still be ways to communicate with the other camps and learn about what is happening in the world. In that regard, I recently bought a commercial grade Wi-Fi router, and I was told to keep the box because I would be taking it with me. It will be used by someone else for a wise purpose.

Once the troubles start, people will not be able to go to a regular temple. There will be portable temples, though, similar to the Tabernacle that was set up in Moses' time.

The third camp I was shown is somewhere in northern New Mexico. I was shown this camp because that is where my parents will be during this time. This is the camp that my mother saw in vision many years ago that I mentioned in an earlier chapter.

This camp is in the midst of many leafy green trees with a lot of water nearby. The protective veil that my mother saw in her dream will be in place to shield the camp from invaders and troublemakers.

Mount Nebo

A fourth location I saw was an observation post near Mount Nebo, the towering peak in Utah between Santaquin and Nephi on the eastern side of I-15. There's a scenic route up there called the Nebo Loop.

I took a solo drive around the loop in October 2014. I had a strong prompting to go up there and see what is available. I have included two photos at the end of this chapter of a location about 8 to 10 miles up the road from the Payson Lakes campground.

When I was there, I felt this will be an observation point for the Saints to watch the valley. I got out of my car and went to the slope. I was alone, but I felt the presence of other men around me who will be there in the near future. They were men who were trained in observation skills, such as hunters and policemen.

I sensed they were behind two or three hunter blinds that you wouldn't be able to see from down in the valley.

They were using large binoculars to track certain groups, then reporting up the chain of command. They must have created a grid of Utah Valley, because they were referring to "x" and "y" coordinates to say such things as, "There's movement in that coordinate. I see tanks and transport carriers."

I sensed there was a camp of Saints somewhere nearby, but this was definitely an observation post.

I saw one of them with a handheld radio, a Midland GXT that I own. They were listening to the transmissions from the enemy, but they didn't ever transmit, so they couldn't be tracked themselves. It was reassuring that the Saints will have people in place, watching the enemy and prepared to defend their people if necessary.

These are two photos from my solo drive around the Nebo Loop on October 2014. The top one shows an elevation sign at the site where I stopped and walked around. Below is the view of Utah Valley from the same location. There is a clear view all the way to the Point of the Mountain.

CHAPTER EIGHT

FINANCIAL COLLAPSE

I believe the first thing we will see after the Saints have gathered to the camps will be the start of the upcoming financial meltdown. My feelings are that it will be caused by the Lord's revocation of our national blessing of protection.

Just before the meltdown becomes fully evident, gasoline prices will soar. I've been having a reoccurring dream where I'm at different gas stations during this time.

In the dream I'm in the process of filling my car when I look up and notice that prices start at $7 a gallon. I also saw prices between $7.00 and $7.65 for unleaded. Each dream is at a different gas station. I've seen Shell, Texaco, Holiday, and Maverik. I wasn't able to see foliage or other ways to indicate the time of the year.

I sensed that people on a fixed income could hardly afford to drive. There were no semis on the street. At the Springville Maverick near I-15, I looked across the street at the Flying J Truck Stop. There were hardly any trucks parked there.

Soon afterward, a financial "release" will happen, and the economic collapse will start then. The effects of that release will be felt soon thereafter (one week to a month). There are a couple of financial instruments that will give us warnings. Those are junk bonds and Treasury Notes.

When one or both of those items start failing, it will signal that the collapse is in play.

The financial release will be so sudden that a large number of people will be left without any financial means. The store shelves will not be stocked, because the trucking industry will come to a halt. There will be no gasoline available, and neither will there be gas for cooking or heating homes.

Most Americans don't have more than a few days' worth of food or supplies in their homes, and it won't take long for people to become desperate. A mob mentality will quickly develop.

An Incident in Chicago

I also saw that the collapse seemed to begin after an incident in Chicago. Unfortunately for everybody, the discord will spread far and wide outside of Chicago.

Looting, carnage, and lawlessness filled the land only a month after whatever economic event had happened. The worst trouble was in the eastern half of the United States, although the West Coast and other major cities were affected.

The people who don't want to fight the mobs will have to leave their cities and towns. Many people will flee to the West from different parts of the United States with nothing more than the clothes on their backs, and holding hands with their children. They will not even have as much as a handcart like the pioneers did.

The Book of Mormon warns us many times that this loss of national protection can happen due to the wickedness of the inhabitants of this land. We are reaching that point.

Part of the reason that things spun out of control is the federal government didn't have power anymore. The dollar was gone. When the collapse first started, a wheelbarrow of money would buy you some food, but after a while no one would take the money.

Even now as I write this in May 2015, the graphs for gold, student loans, the dollar currency, stocks, and oil are all "frothy." They look like precursors of a troubling economic event. The Chinese and the Russians have recently completed trade agreements that will allow them to trade in their own currency. They can completely bypass the dollar, which would leave the United States in a dire situation.

When the dollar is devalued or the stock market crashes, the federal government won't have the tools that it had in the past to handle the situation.

This was made clear to me in a vision. I was looking down on the map of the United States, and a voice said, "Look there."

My eyes were drawn to the Washington D.C. area. There were protests in the streets and violent clashes between the citizens and police officers. The recent problems in Ferguson, Missouri and Baltimore, Maryland seemed like a minor playground spat compared to the ugly destruction and deaths I witnessed there.

In one scene I saw the local police completely overwhelmed, so the National Guard was called in, but even they couldn't contain the violence.

I understood that the White House actually ordered the National Guard to openly shoot citizens, but they wouldn't do it. So the government called in the U.S. Army, but even they seemed shorthanded to stop the rioting and killing.

Finally the United Nations volunteered their peacekeepers to assist us, and martial law was officially declared in several areas of the country. I saw men from England, France, and other countries among these U.N. peacekeepers, who all wore blue helmets. I have seen these peacekeepers in several different dreams.

The U.N. tried to establish peace, and they did in some areas, but the plagues that I described earlier were beginning to rage throughout the nation.

The biggest shock to me was how violent it got, and so quickly. Even being aware of the prophecies concerning the last days, it still shocked me how rapidly society fell apart. It made me sick to my stomach. There will be indiscriminate killing, even kids killing kids. I dream in all five senses, so unfortunately when I am shown these scenes I can smell the blood in the streets and sense the fear in the citizens' hearts.

The United Nations peacekeepers set up safe zones in some of the cities. Long concrete blocks were put in place, along with anti-tank defenses. It seemed like overkill, but they were frightened that the rampaging citizens might unite and fight them.

Government Factions Emerge

Despite the national troubles, a U.S. presidential

election had still been held. A new president had been elected, but hadn't taken office yet. It soon became clear that it would never happen, because amid the turmoil a lot of different groups were claiming to be in charge, and the old administration didn't want to give up power. I sensed that Congress itself broke into different factions, and Washington D.C. was abandoned due to the violence there.

The United Nations played a major role in enforcing martial law, and Denver, Colorado became a pseudo national capital, with a heavy U.N. presence there.

I was shown a scene from high above the country. I was moving very fast from city to city. I saw many large cities such as New York City, Pittsburgh, and Boston, and they were all filled with rioting, looting, and killing.

Martial law would be implemented nationwide. In one vivid dream I saw soldiers holding semi-automatic weapons as they rounded people up to insert an RFID chip in them to be able to track their whereabouts. A large mass of people had been herded into a huge warehouse. One door was open, and people were funneled into a single-file line as they left the warehouse.

I was standing outside on what was once a grassy area, but the grass had died. Now it was just dirt. Soldiers were standing there using a pneumatic gun to put the RFID chip into people. They typically put it in a person's hand.

Then I saw a man reach the front of the line who was in his mid-30s. He wouldn't approach the workers. He said, "I don't want to get it."

Suddenly a man came from behind him and put

him in a half-nelson wrestling hold. Then two other guys hurried forward to hold him down. As the man was squirming in the dirt to get free, another worker came forward and put the pneumatic gun to the man's forehead and pulled the trigger.

The dream thankfully ended there.

CHAPTER NINE

MY PERSONAL ASSIGNMENT

I mentioned earlier about how there are waves of people already beginning to move in various directions to fulfill the Lord's purposes. These waves will continue when the prophet invites the Saints to gather to places of refuge.

Unfortunately, the waves of people that come after that won't be the ones who willingly and obediently made changes in their lives.

The last few waves of people are the ones who were unprepared and are now desperate to simply stay alive. They will be forced out of their homes and will be trying to avoid the violence. There will be many good people among this group who will be guided to the places of refuge in the Rocky Mountains.

We need to open our hearts to those less fortunate than we are. Charity is what these people will need from us, not the giving of things, but the giving of our hearts. They will need the balm of welcoming to heal them from the horrors they have seen and suffered.

That is what my mission will be during this time. Once I have made sure my children and other family members are safe in a place of refuge, my wife and I will return to the valley to lead people to safety when the full wrath of the Lord is poured out on this nation. It is a humbling task that we are already preparing for.

Women and Children on the Railroad Tracks

The following dream is one I first received after my family had moved to Enterprise, Utah when I was around 15 years old. At the time, the dream made little sense to me, but now it does.

In this dream I was a grown man. It was daytime, and the trees around me were green with leaves. It was early summer by the way the trees looked. I was kneeling down examining railroad tracks to see whether they were being used. The tracks were rusted and looked overgrown with weeds.

I had on hiking boots and a long-sleeve shirt with the sleeves rolled up. I had a small daypack. It felt like I was doing reconnaissance work, checking things out. The dream was so vivid I could smell the railroad ties.

While I was examining the tracks, I felt eyes on me. I looked up and saw a group of people in the distance. I wasn't alarmed at their appearance, so I stood up and stayed in place while the group came closer.

I noticed that there were no men among them, but I somehow knew there were 26 women and several children. Everybody looked disheveled. They were strung out along the tracks. They looked like they had been sleeping in the dirt.

One lady in her late 50s approached me. She was wearing a red blouse, dark trousers and what was left of some heeled shoes. The shoes no longer had the heels. She was holding hands with a young boy. They both looked very unkempt. Their faces were very dusty and their hair was sticking out at many angles.

The woman said, "We have come from back East, and we didn't have time to pack anything. We heard that there was peace in the West where the Mormons are." That's where this dream always ends.

Marauders Looking for Us

I feel this dream is related to one that both my mother and I had. In the dream it was at night, and I was with a group of people in a mountain canyon filled with conifer trees. Judging by the appearance of the rocks and the granular clay soil, I would guess I was somewhere in Spanish Fork Canyon in Utah.

I felt like I was patrolling outside of a camp near a stream. I was walking along the tree line, where the conifers turned into bushes. I could hear movements coming from below me. They were using a big stick to try to fight their way through the thicket.

I sensed three marauders who were feeling desperate to find us and our food. They were very determined to find us. They were cussing in frustration and saying unpleasant things.

A man shouted, "Keep searching! The Mormons have got to be here somewhere."

The other men kept saying things like, "Yeah, they've got to be here."

I sat down and stayed silent, listening to them. Finally after about twenty minutes, they gave up. Their clothes were being torn by the thicket, so they headed back down the canyon.

A Jet Crash

A couple of years ago, I had a fragment of a dream that has disturbed me. I've had this one frequently enough to remember a lot of details.

My wife and I had come back to our neighborhood as part of our assignment to make sure that everybody was out. I can't tell if we drove there or were dropped off. I feel that the rest of the family was safe and in the mountains already. We were on our last mission to gather stragglers.

We were walking south on a road. It was dusk and the trees didn't have leaves. Weirdly, some grass on people's front yards was still green in patches. It felt like early fall. My wife and I were carrying large backpacks and wearing hiking boots.

I didn't see any cars parked on the road. There were quite a few piles of leaves on the front yards and on the road. There was a little bit of wind, but it wasn't very cold yet. I was wearing a long sleeve T-shirt and had a fleece sweater tied around my waist.

We reached 1600 South in Springville and were about to turn east toward the mountains, when I heard a loud rushing sound. A few seconds later a two-engine passenger jet smashed into the ground. The plane came from the south, so I think it was en route to the nearest airport.

It crashed on its left side, and the whole side was crumpled. The right wing was up in the air for a few seconds. Then a fireball shot into the sky.

We would have rushed to help the passengers, but

the flames were too intense, and we knew there were no survivors. After watching the plane burn for a couple minutes, we continued east toward the mountains.

Everyone Plays a Role

Everyone has specific gifts. Some people are experts at emergency preparedness. Others have the talents to deal with long-term survival. My gifts are to receive communications from heaven, to create spiritual and emotional safe havens, and to lead people to spiritual and temporal safety.

This feels like an appropriate place to share a very special vision I had in February 2015 that gave me clarity about each of our roles here on earth.

I was thinking about our era, how much suffering and sadness is happening. I thought and pondered about the War in Heaven, and wondered what part I played there. My mind was drawn to the meeting between Abraham and the Lord in the pre-mortal world that is described in the scriptures.

Abraham 3:22-23 reads, "Now the Lord had shown unto me, Abraham, the intelligences that were organized before the world was; and among all these there were many of the noble and great ones;

"And God saw these souls that they were good, and he stood in the midst of them, and he said: These I will make my rulers; for he stood among those that were spirits, and he saw that they were good; and he said unto me: Abraham, thou art one of them; thou wast chosen before thou wast born."

As I read those verses, my understanding was opened, and the Spirit of the Lord rested upon me. I saw the following scene:

After the meeting with the noble and great ones that Abraham described, the Lord approached a large group I was with. There were millions of us there, and we were all wearing white robes.

We gathered around the Lord. I was about ten feet from him. He extended his right hand and started speaking. He expressed his gratitude for us being there. He turned to his left, and pointed behind him to the previous group he had spoken to. He then said, "I have chosen them to be the leaders in your mortal trial. However, I did not choose you. You have chosen me."

He then proceeded to compare the different groups, which were many, to his body. He said that the leaders in the other group were the head of his body. However, he said we were his hands and feet. We would do his work and hold up the body of Christ, meaning both the Church and its members.

He called us "The Hands of the Lord." We were so excited! We started speaking amongst ourselves, eager to get to work on our assignments.

The Lord gently called out to us, "I am not done speaking with you."

We quieted down and looked at him intently. He proceeded to explain that we were essential to our Father's Plan. He would need to sprinkle us through the different ages of earth's history so that we could help the Lord accomplish his purposes.

He then turned in my direction and said to us, "I will send my pillars to prepare my way for my coming in glory in the last dispensation. You will be my soldiers to contain the evil that will arise in your lifetimes. You will be the bulwark that will create safe havens from this rising tide of evil. You will raise families and children that will be faithful to the plan. You will do all the mundane things that are needful and right. While these things are not exciting and glamorous, these are the things that will form the bedrock upon which the foundation of righteousness will be built."

There were millions of us there, and we could all hear the voice of the Savior. I'm not sure how this was done, but he proceeded to speak of many other things. He even showed us how we will recognize each other. This would be revealed to us at the appropriate time.

The Spirit of the Lord retired and the vision ended.

It was wonderful to realize the Lord knows each of us, and we each have a role to play in these final days before the Second Coming.

CHAPTER TEN

CONCENTRATION
CAMPS ON U.S. SOIL

Through these dreams and visions, I have a firm grasp of what the danger will be for many U.S. citizens. I've also had some very disturbing views into the future of Utah that have left me very angry at the secret combinations and what they are planning to do.

Through revelation, I was shown that my name, my wife's name, and a daughter's name have been put on a watch list for potential "troublemakers and rabble-rousers."

The list is being compiled by a federal agency that is allied with the National Security Agency. This group is keeping tabs on people through social media and other methods.

This agency is counting on people feeling safe in expressing their opinions openly. Make no mistake, anybody that even "smells" like trouble will be on that list. This is part of the reason why the Church and our leaders are keeping a low profile. They don't want to tip their hand and have people rounded up before the right time to gather to the places of refuge.

Just as the Church is preparing places of refuge, the federal government is preparing concentration camps for so-called troublemakers. I know this sounds absurd, but when martial law is enacted, the justice system will go by the wayside. Having your "day in court" will be a thing of the past. Judgment will be made quickly and harshly.

I was shown camps that will be built in the desert between I-15 and Tooele, among other places, such as Herriman and the Cedar Valley. They were built about a mile apart along highways for easy transportation.

These camps were more like outdoor holding pens. They will have 12-foot-high concrete-slab walls with razor sharp barb-wire on the top. There were no barracks, toilet facilities, or shelter provided of any kind. It was just dirt and weeds inside. There was no privacy at all.

The enclosure usually had five or six sides, and were very long and rectangular, with only one entrance. There were guard towers on the corners, and barracks outside for the guards.

Once these structures were built, the government began rounding people up. These were the people that stayed behind and were on this list I mentioned before. The sun beat on them, and rain fell on them. It was the Nazi camps all over again. People were just thrown in these enclosures without so much as water.

I saw black vans with a yellow logo stopping at the entrances, and the guards would hurriedly drag the occupants out and toss them into the enclosure. There were men, women and children being imprisoned.

Many of these people were relatives of those that left for the mountains. These evil taskmasters were using these people as pawns, trying to get the Saints to come back down and rescue them. They were doing radio broadcasts and dropping leaflets over the mountains telling what was happening. In the cities, neighbors would report any hint of suspicious activity to gain the favor of the government. It was despicable.

I didn't see all of the enclosures and their locations, only the ones where my relatives were being held. It makes me sad to even think about it.

CHAPTER ELEVEN

THE SECOND EARTHQUAKE

Once the Saints have departed from the Wasatch Front and are safely at the places of refuge, a second earthquake will strike Utah. This one will be much more powerful than the first one.

The damage I saw was almost unbelievable. The shaking will be so dramatic that landslides will roar down the mountain faces. I could hardly fathom the sheer volume of dirt and rocks that will engulf the homes along the benches and bury them. The mountains looked bare where the houses had been.

Every canyon will be cut off due to the landslides. It will be similar to when the monstrous Thistle landslide happened in the early 1980s in Spanish Fork Canyon that buried the highway and blocked the river. But this time there will be dozens of slides that size along the Wasatch Front, and many of the slides will be bigger.

The devastation near the Point of the Mountain was probably the worst. I saw the towering sign along I-15 that reads, "Outlets: Traverse Mountain" fall south onto its face.

In that same area, the earth will literally collapse into a giant sinkhole. The Timpanogos Highway was really broken up and impassible. I saw that all of the brand new buildings in the Thanksgiving Point area were severely damaged. Thousands of windows were shattered. The sandy soil in the area had basically liquefied, and many of the buildings simply disappeared like they were in quicksand. Others were half-buried and on fire.

I sensed there was tremendous terror and discord among the people who were there, but I wasn't shown the actual people, because I didn't ask.

A Terrible Flood

Several years ago I had a waking vision that is related to this second earthquake.

I was working in an office building that is near the mouth of Provo Canyon. After work, I went to my car in the parking lot. Then I had another of those experiences where a future event is superimposed over my actual surroundings.

I heard a rushing sound coming toward me. I looked toward Provo Canyon. There is a hydroelectric pressure box near the top of the north canyon wall that has penstock pipes coming out of it, and I saw a wall of brown water shoot out of the canyon at that height. It had to have been almost 100 feet high. The water crashed into the ridge that leads to Orem, and then it funneled down the river bed toward Provo.

Within seconds the water reached me. It was dark chocolate brown and filled with debris such as an uprooted pine tree. I could smell the earthy aroma as it swirled around me.

Before I knew it, the water was over my head and I was swept away. I sensed I was going to drown.

Suddenly the vision shifted and I was in the south

This is a view of the mouth of Provo Canyon below Mount Timpanogos. In my vision I saw the flood waters shooting out of the canyon at the height of the pressure box along the cliff on the left side of the photo.

end of Provo known as East Bay. The water had spread throughout the city and was about four feet deep in this area. There was devastation everywhere, with tons of debris being deposited there.

I realized that the water had come from the Jordanelle and Deer Creek reservoirs. The earthquake had damaged the dams and sent all that water cascading down the canyon.

I sensed that the water had inundated parts of Springville, Spanish Fork, and other cities near Utah Lake, which was now several feet deeper. The water had covered my yard in west Springville, but my house is slightly elevated, so it didn't go in the house.

Provo and Orem were now disaster zones after the earthquake and the flood, and thousands of people wanted to get out of there. They couldn't go north, though, because of the problems at the Point of the Mountain, and the canyons were blocked, so their only option was to head south. Due to the flooding in Provo, the only clear route was along U.S. Highway 89 over Ironton Hill into Springville.

Citizens Stopped from Leaving

I had another vision that is related to this situation. One day I had a strong feeling to go outside. I stepped out onto my back porch, and a vision opened up. I heard what sounded like C-130s flying in the sky above north Springville, but they looked like a Chinese version of troop carriers.

I counted four jets, going west to east. They were dropping more than a dozen paratroopers along the north edge of Springville. They had circular parachutes, and only two nations have them, the U.S. and Chinese. They were wearing dark olive uniforms.

These paratroopers landed and then stationed themselves at the intersection of 1400 North and Main street in Springville, near the McDonalds. They had one mission. They were stopping people from traveling south. If anyone objected or tried to get past them, they would be shot.

Then the vision closed.

CHAPTER TWELVE

THE INVASION FROM FOREIGN TROOPS

All of the troubles and confusion in the United Sates during this time will leave the country vulnerable. Everyone will be so wrapped up in their own problems that they won't even consider that other countries might see us as easy prey.

I've had some dreams and visions related to the Chinese invading America, but they seemed disjointed at the time. So I've been doing a lot of reading and investigating.

A surprise attack is the best strategy. Pearl Harbor, 9-11, and several others prove this, but how are the Chinese going to be able to move so many troops on the western and southern coasts? The answer is they already have their strategy underway.

For several years now, the Chinese have been paying for improvements in most of the West Coast deep-water ports. These include the Panama Canal, and ones in California and Washington. The way they will surprise the U.S. is by putting troops, tanks, and helicopters into containers on those large transport ships.

I saw massive amounts of troops and equipment pour out of these ships into different ports on the U.S. West Coast. I saw several others dock in northwestern Mexico and made a push through Arizona. This will happen after the U.N. informs them that the time is right. There will be spies embedded in the U.N. forces, and they will communicate back to China the following message: "There's no resistance, come take it."

There is a reason the Chinese are so prominent in invasion dreams. Apparently, there will be a very large engagement on the air and sea between the United States and Russia. This war will cripple Russia and turn their forces into mainly a land-based military. It will also deplete the U.S. army and navy, and leave the country exposed to a takeover.

The Chinese will wisely stay out of the U.S.-Russia conflict. The Russian military will have a smaller role than the Chinese in this part of the world.

I saw that this Chinese invasion happens some time after the Saints have gone to the places of refuge and have left Babylon behind. I don't know how long after, only that the Saints will be made aware that they are conquering the country.

A Warning for Southern Arizona

One morning I said my morning prayer, as usual, then jumped in the shower. I was thinking about my son, who is attending a major university in Arizona. He is staying with my sister's family near the university.

While I was thinking on how to give him advanced warning to get out (he's skeptical about calamities happening in his lifetime), a vision opened up in my mind. Whether I was seeing it with my natural eyes or my spiritual eyes, I cannot tell.

I was above Arizona, and I saw what looked like a map below me. The map zoomed to southern Arizona, where I could see Tucson, and part of northern Mexico.

I saw that Mexico was a different color than the United States. While I was looking at the map, I saw the colored portion of Mexico changing along the border so that it appeared that Mexico's region was expanding northward. I felt a prompting to look east of Tucson, and I saw that the eastern routes to New Mexico were cut off.

The color of Mexico now covered the eastern portion of I-10. Only I-10 north was open. There was a pause in the northward march of the color, then it quickly covered Tucson and went toward the Phoenix metro area.

I did not see nor was I told the meaning of the change of color, only that the people there must flee from it. I didn't see what happened to Phoenix because the map darkened before I could see it reaching Phoenix. I did see the color reach Phoenix's southern metro areas, though. It had taken over Casa Grande and the town of Maricopa. It looked like it was heading toward Gilbert and Chandler when the map darkened.

I saw that the towns of Bisbee, Sierra Vista, Benson, Tombstone, Wilcox, and St. David were all taken over by the color change. Surprisingly, the color stopped going east before it got to San Simon. What I saw were two spearhead movements, one from Douglas and another from Nogales.

Whatever the color change represented, it left Gila Valley alone. It looked like the color changes were occurring mostly in metropolitan areas. The activity on the map I saw only went up to the Phoenix metro area. I do know that Snowflake, Show Low, Pinetop-Lakeside, and Mt. Graham are areas of refuge.

After this vision, I had a very specific prompting to mail copies of my house keys to my sister and my son.

It looks like they will flee to Utah but will become separated, but they will both eventually make it to my house. I was told that the stored water and food I already have is for them and a few other people. I was told I would already be gone from the house by the time they get there.

I saw that because of my future assignment to assist others who were still in the valley, I would be able to go back and find them there, then take them to safety.

I wasn't given a specific timeline concerning these Arizona developments other than they will happen during or shortly after the gathering of the Saints has taken place.

CHAPTER THIRTEEN

GLOBAL NATURAL DISASTERS

During this time, there will also be many natural disasters across the world. I have seen one specific disaster that relates directly to Puerto Rico.

I started having this dream shortly after coming to Utah in 1982. I was 15 at the time. It happened after I got my patriarchal blessing. I've had this dream many times since then, but I recently had an expanded version of this dream.

The updated dream came after I had been studying about the upcoming earthquakes in America. I had an experience I can only describe as having my eyes opened to a greater understanding of what I had seen in dreams thus far.

I feel I should first share the version of the dream that I've had for years, then I will add the latest information.

It started with me in an airplane leaving Puerto Rico going west toward Florida. We were about 35,000 feet in the air, the usual cruising altitude for commercial airlines. I found myself floating stationary at that altitude, looking back toward the island. The clouds at the altitude were wispy so I could see the shape of the island clearly.

I was looking almost straight down and eastward when I saw an enormous wave traveling east to west. It first swallowed several of the smaller Antilles that are southeast of Puerto Rico. I watched as the bow of the wave passed over Puerto Rico and the island disappeared from sight.

I watched the wave wash over the Dominican Republic, Haiti, Jamaica, and Cuba. They were all swallowed up by the wave. I saw several other waves heading northwest toward the East Coast of the United States.

Then I woke up. I've had this dream quite a few times the past thirty years.

Now here is the latest information I have received.

This time the dream started on the Canary Islands, off the coast of northern Africa. There was a large quake, and the western side of the Cumbre Vieja volcano fell into the sea. There was an enormous tsunami spreading out westward and northward from the Canary Islands.

I was still watching from the air. I saw a large bulge of water pushing upward and the waves spreading. I watched the southern half of the wave swallow up the Caribbean islands and the Gulf of Mexico. The northern part of the wave hit Florida and up to Nova Scotia and Greenland. Many cities were swallowed up by the first wave and the subsequent ones. The tsunami wave flooded inland several miles. The entire eastern coastline was changed.

I've been trying to get as many of my family members to leave those areas, but the majority are still there. I do find it interesting that many LDS Church members from the island have come to the U.S. mainland in recent years.

A Third Earthquake

I feel the dream involving the tsunami is part of a worldwide earthquake that will take place. I have mentioned two earthquakes that will strike Utah, but there will eventually be a third one that will devastate both North and South America at the same time. This will be the true Big One. Not much will be left standing or intact. There are several things that have to happen before this one comes. I don't know the full timeline on this earthquake, other than it will happen before New Jerusalem is built.

I was shown some of the effects of this earthquake. Both coasts of the United States had changed shape. Most of southern Florida was underwater.

California looked very different than it looks today. Most of southern California was underwater, and there were a few islands in the ocean where Los Angeles had been. I looked at a map afterward, and it looks like anything west of the San Andreas Fault had dropped into the ocean.

Also, the Mississippi River basin will widen greatly because of the earthquake. There will be an expanse of water several miles wide from the Great Lakes all the way to the Gulf of Mexico. This will in effect divide the country in half.

CHAPTER FOURTEEN

ZION WILL PREVAIL

As terrible as these upcoming events will be, there is a great purpose in it for the cleansing of America. It is to prepare the land for the establishment of Zion, and the construction of the New Jerusalem. The Saints living in the places of refuge will be aware of this, and they will be eagerly awaiting the opportunity.

The Chinese army will still be occupying the country, but as the Saints get word of the Chinese invasion, there will be a movement within the places of refuge to rally the righteous of this nation to beat back the invaders, and to have our flag fly over our ramparts again.

The Elders of Israel will battle for freedom, and they will emerge triumphantly.

A Vision of Battle

In regard to that battle, I recently received a special gift on my birthday. As I lay in bed that morning, I was awake and thinking about the many things I needed to do. I was finally able to relax and my mind was opened.

I heard a herald announcing: "Repent ye, repent ye O House of Israel. Repent ye, repent ye O House of Jacob, Repent ye, repent ye O House of Ephraim! The Lord's anger is kindled and none shall deliver! Make way, make way, for the Lord's coming is nigh!"

The vision continued with me being transported

into a field of battle. It was dark from all the smoke. The smell of ammunition smoke was very heavy. I couldn't really see around me that much. There were sharp cracks of weapons being fired around me. I heard machine guns, rifles, and howitzers. I felt the ground shake from artillery shells falling around me. I also heard many people screaming and moaning in pain. I wasn't afraid, but mostly sad that this was taking place.

The sounds of battle faded away. It was still very dark. I then felt the dirt beneath my feet shake. There was a loud and prolonged growl, like a deep rumble. I also started hearing the high-pitched sound you hear when you bang two rocks together. It was a very intense sound that went on for what appeared a couple minutes.

The sounds of the earth faded away, and I found myself with my wife on a dirt path, just outside a large tent. This was the largest tent I had ever seen. I stepped inside, and noticed that there was a lot of light inside. I noticed that there was a seat like a throne at the back of the tent.

I walked toward it to see who was there. As I got closer, I realized who was sitting there. I noticed that he was wearing a white robe, with a tan cape and leather sandals.

I ran up a couple steps to him. He stood up and I threw my arms around him and gave him a bear hug. While I was hugging him, I said, "Oh Brother, how I missed you!"

I could feel him smiling. I let go of the bear hug and looked into his eyes. He put his arm around my shoulders and pulled me closer. He pointed outward with his free arm and said, "I am very happy that you made it here. Many of your brothers and sisters have not made it here yet. Please go out and bring them here to me."

Then I wake up. Here's the greatest testimony I can give—He lives!

We are soldiers continuing the war in heaven. We are being awakened!

Onward, Christian soldiers!
Marching as to war,
With the cross of Jesus
Going on before.

Miracles and Healings

During this war, the power of the priesthood will be strongly evident. In one dream I saw a group of our people who were lying dead when we approached them. Through the power of the priesthood they were raised from the dead. They stood up under their own power, blinked, and asked, "What happened?"

This happened many times. I was shown a panorama of these miracles, like little snippets of video showing different miracles and healings.

Then the video seemed to expand so I couldn't see the end of it. It was a testimony to me that the power of God will be in full operation as the cause of Zion goes forth.

There were other types of miracles. I saw a whole mountain picked up and moved in order to fulfill the Lord's purposes. Such things will be common among the

Saints as their faith grows and their various situations require it.

Starting Over

Once the war is over and peace begins to settle on the land, there will still be many non-LDS Americans in the land. The Saints will reach out to them and help them.

I was shown an interesting vision that pertains to that. I was standing on a prairie where there was a 30-foot storage unit that seemed to be functioning like a field hospital.

There was an older couple there talking to several people in their late 20s or early 30s. There was a pile of electronic gadgets outside, such as iPhones, tablets, and so on. The younger people were sorting through them, trying to switch them on, but nothing would work. Even after the war, they still longed for these gadgets.

Finally the older lady told them, "You don't need those things now."

Her husband motioned to the group and said, "Come with me. I'll teach you how to farm, and provide for yourselves."

The young people seemed surprised at such an idea, but they eventually followed him. It just showed me how things are going to change in so many ways.

CHAPTER FIFTEEN

PERSONAL PREPAREDNESS

I hope it is clear that I am a strong believer in 72-hour kits for each member of the family. Below is a list of items to store in a 72-hour kit to help you be prepared in the case of an emergency.

In one dream, I was then shown to put our blue tarps, toilet paper, and other personal hygiene products in one of the large plastic bins that we have. Next I was shown an animation of a large transparent Ziploc bag. I saw a toothbrush, toothpaste, soap, and deodorant go in one by one.

Next came a checklist for every bag, and that it needed to go in a sheet protector. This was to go in the large bag as well. Each person in the family will need to have this bag as part of their bug out bag.

My wife and I have been shown specific items about every two to three days. We have purchased hiking boots and backpacks for the family. We also have 72-hour kits for each member of the family. We are continuing to prepare and purchase different items as we feel impressed to do so.

This kit should be put together in a practical manner so that you can carry it with you if you ever need to evacuate your home. It is also important to prepare one for each member of your family who is able to carry one. There are several similar lists on the Internet.

Food and Water

A three-day supply of food and water, per person, when no refrigeration or cooking is available.
- Protein/Granola Bars
- Trail Mix/Dried Fruit
- Crackers/Cereals (for munching)
- Canned Tuna, Beans, Turkey, Beef, Vienna Sausages, etc.
- Canned Juice
- Candy/Gum
- Water (1 Gallon/4 Liters Per Person)

Bedding and Clothing

- Change of Clothing (short and long sleeved shirts, pants, jackets, socks, etc.)
- Undergarments
- Rain Coat/Poncho
- Blankets and Emergency Heat Blanks (that keep in warmth)
- Cloth Sheet
- Plastic Sheet

Fuel and Light

- Battery Lighting (Flashlights, Lamps, etc.)
- Extra Batteries
- Flares
- Candles
- Lighter
- Water-Proof Matches

Other Equipment

- Can Opener
- Dishes/Utensils
- Shovel
- Radio (with batteries!)
- Pen and Paper
- Axe
- Pocket Knife
- Rope
- Duct Tape

Personal Supplies and Medication

- First Aid Kit and Supplies
- Toiletries (roll of toilet paper- remove the center tube to easily flatten into a zip-lock bag, feminine hygiene, folding brush, etc.)
- Cleaning Supplies (mini hand sanitizer, soap, shampoo, dish soap, etc. Warning: Scented soap might "flavor" food items.)
- Immunizations Up-to Date
- Medication (Acetaminophen, Ibuprofen, children's medication etc.)
- Prescription Medication (for three days)

Personal Documents and Money

(Place these items in a water-proof container!)
- Scriptures
- Genealogy Records
- Vaccination Papers

- Legal Documents (Birth/Marriage Certificates, Wills, Passports, Contracts, etc)
- Insurance Policies
- Cash
- Credit Card
- Pre-Paid Phone Cards
- Bags to put 72-hour kit items in (such as duffel bags or back packs, which work great). Make sure you can lift and carry it!
- Infant Needs (if applicable)

Additional Thoughts

1. Update your 72-hour kit every six months (put a note in your calendar/planner) to make sure that: all food, water, and medication is fresh and has not expired; clothing fits; personal documents and credit cards are up to date; and batteries are charged.

2. Small toys/games are important too as they will provide some comfort and entertainment during a stressful time.

3. Older children can be responsible for their own pack of items/clothes too.

4. You can include any other items in your 72-hour kit that you feel are necessary for your family's survival.

5. Some items and/or flavors might leak, melt, "flavor" other items, or break open. Dividing groups of items into individual Ziploc bags might help prevent this.

We have augmented our kits to deal with my dietary needs. We have also added stuff like fire starters, collapsible cups, plates, utensils, pocket knives, and can openers.

We have purchased hiking backpacks for each family member so we can carry more. Regular backpacks carry the weight on your shoulders. Hiking backpacks put the load on your hips, meaning that you will walk further with the same weight and won't be as tired.

Here's the list of stuff that I have been directed to get for my family:

- Hiking boots, socks, and backpacks
- Hygiene kits for each person
- Freeze-dried food packs for each backpack
- As many two-man tents as possible, avoiding the flimsy tube tents that come in the basic 72-hour kits sold online.
- A few blue 55-gallon drums to store water

Remember that this list is very specific to my family. Your preparations will need to be tailored to your situation and what the Holy Spirit is telling you to do.

I am grateful for the love and support of my wife Tammy, above, and my parents, shown below.

CHAPTER SIXTEEN

My Testimony

Make preparations for your family and live your life. Trust in the Lord. He will protect us as long as we are listening to the Spirit. I'm just a man and my current priesthood stewardship is over my family and the families I home teach.

Religious and temporal direction rightly belongs to our appointed leaders, such as the Prophet, Apostles, bishoprics, stake presidencies, seventies, area presidencies, and other general authorities. I exhort you to cultivate prayer, and listening to the Spirit.

Throughout the scriptures, we are promised that we shall receive answers. However it is up to us to do the asking. Heavenly Father is eager to tell you wonderful things and to give you instructions in anything that you ask of him. We are literally his sons and daughters. It is our divine right to get answers. We just have to be courageous enough to claim this right for ourselves.

I encourage you to prepare your family to be able to make it through this event.

A change is coming.

CHAPTER SEVENTEEN

A Warning Vision

This chapter is an unexpected last-minute addition to the book. When I received the following vision, the manuscript had been typeset and was essentially ready to go to press. But my publisher and I felt this vision should be included, due to the details it contains and the urgency I felt as I experienced it.

I had this vision while I was at work one morning in early May 2015. I had been pondering about the recent riots in Baltimore, Maryland. I was also thinking about a prophecy attributed to Joseph Smith that indicates the United States' second civil war will start in Chicago over monetary devaluation.

I was thinking deeply about these things when my surroundings changed. I was no longer in my office space. Instead, I was in the middle of a large crowd in a distant U.S. city.

I was on a sidewalk with many other people. In front of me I saw young black folks in T-shirts. I vividly remember the guy in front of me wearing a red T-shirt.

To my right were cars parked along the road. To my left was a building wall. I was being pushed along by a crowd going forward on the sidewalk. This looked like a typical residential neighborhood close to the city center, but I have no idea which city it was.

There was a palpable sense of fear, anger, and frustration among the people that surrounded me. They were in the road and on the opposite sidewalk as well.

I heard snippets of a few nearby conversations. Some people were talking about finding food, while others were talking about several stores that had already been cleaned out.

There was an angry buzz throughout the crowd when people started talking about going to the richer suburbs to get food. I had been walking with the crowd for a while, and I noticed we had reached an area that was much nicer than where I was when the vision began. The road was not patched up like in the earlier area, and there was actually grass between the curb and the sidewalk.

We reached a nice suburb where the homes were surrounded by iron fences. The people started climbing these fences in droves to loot the homes.

The next thing I knew it was evening. The sun was going down. There was a big commotion up ahead of me, and the crowd rushed forward. I found myself in the middle of a very large and violent melee. I felt something strike me on the right side of my face, then on the bridge of my nose. My eyesight turned black, and I felt myself hit the sidewalk, landing on my side.

A View from Above

I opened my eyes, and I was several thousand feet in the air above southern Utah and northern Arizona. I was looking east. I saw pillars of smoke rising from cities all across the land. The eastern seaboard had a thick haze covering it. I learned that rioting was happening in many cities at the same time. I looked toward Texas and saw a few pillars of smoke, but nothing like what I saw along the East Coast.

I turned around to look at the West Coast. Southern California had a thick haze blowing out to the west. The haze thinned out heading northward about halfway up the state. The U.S. Northwest was also covered in smoky haze.

I looked down and noticed some smoke rising from Salt Lake City, but it was nothing like the other cities across the United States. In the West, the Phoenix metro area had the most smoke. Las Vegas had about the same amount of smoke as Salt Lake City.

Newspaper Headlines

I closed my eyes, and when I opened them again, I was looking at the front page of a newspaper. I wasn't able to see what the name of the newspaper was. Only the news stories themselves were clear.

One headline read: "New York Stock Exchange closes due to rapid drop in stock values."

To my right, I saw a TV showing footage of a news anchorman talking about the electronic safeguards kicking in on Wall Street and halting trading.

The anchorman said that after the third time this safeguard had been triggered, officials decided to stop trading at the New York Stock Exchange. I was made aware this had happened on a Monday.

The newspaper and the TV news changed quickly

to Tuesday. It was repeat of Monday. The newspaper and TV footage then switched to Wednesday, when the world was told the stock exchange was closed until further notice.

The talking heads on the TV news shows were all trying to put a positive spin on the bad news, but few people were buying their lies anymore.

Everything shifted forward to Friday. I ignored the TV news and looked at the newspaper. One big headline read: "Bankruptcies Announced."

I looked closer and saw a fairly long list of companies closing their doors. I was extremely surprised to see some very well-known companies on that list. I saw Bank of America, Goldman Sachs, and JP Morgan.

I saw a blurb about Wells Fargo closing several divisions, but that the company was not completely going under. There were many other company names mentioned in the article that I did not recognize.

I spotted another headline that read: "300K Out of Work."

The newspaper moved away to my left and out of my sight. Then the TV moved directly in front of me. I stepped back as other TVs moved around the first TV, until I was facing a full wall of TVs.

Each TV was playing a different snippet of what was happening in regard to this financial crisis. There was too much information being thrown at me, and I was barely able to understand all of the voices talking.

The little bits and pieces I caught were very disturbing. Whole industries were shutting down, forcing tens of thousands of people out of work overnight. The most worrisome aspect, at least to me, was that many transportation companies simply stopped operating. They just turned off the lights and posted notices on their doors that they were out of business. This caused massive disruptions to all types of deliveries that were scheduled in the cities.

The people in the nation's rural areas fared much better, but they still suffered the effects of the financial meltdown.

This event will be known as Obsidian Monday, and it will happen soon. It will be a dark and sharp dagger that will cut out the heart of the American economy. Moloch is getting his sacrifice and his pound of flesh.

This is the small, simple headstone of Charles D. Evans, located in the Historic Springville City Cemetery. He saw many of the same events concerning the last days that I have seen. I now live about a mile from his burial site.

APPENDIX

THE VISION OF
CHARLES D. EVANS

When I was a young man soon after joining the LDS Church, I was having many dreams that were confusing to me. Around 1989 I read the following vision that was received by Patriarch Charles D. Evans. It meant a lot to me when I first read it, because it showed that someone else had seen the same things I had.

Patriarch Evans lived in Springville, Utah, just as I do now, and his vision was published in 1894 in *The Contributor* magazine, an early LDS Church publication.

This vision has since been published in many places, but I hope it will be beneficial to those who may not have read it before.

Here is the vision:

"A Dream" by Charles D. Evans

While I lay pondering, in deep solitude, on the events of the present my mind was drawn into a reverie such as I had never felt before. A strong solicitude for my imperilled country utterly excluded every other thought and raised my feelings to a point of intensity I did not think it possible to endure.

While in this solemn, profound, and painful reverie

of mind, to my infinite surprise, a light appeared in my room, which seemed to be soft and silvery as that diffused from a northern star. At the moment of its appearance the acute feeling I had experienced instantly yielded to one of calm tranquility.

Although it may have been at the hour of midnight, and the side of the globe whereon I was situated, was excluded from the sunlight, yet all was light and bright and warm as an Italian landscape at noon; but the heat was softer or more subdued.

As I gazed upward, I saw descending through my bedroom roof, with a gently gliding movement, a personage clothed in white apparel, whose countenance was smoothly serene, his features regular, and the flashes of his eye seemed to shoot forth scintillations, to use an earthly comparison, strongly resembling those reflected from a diamond under an intensely illumined electric light, which dazzled but did not bewilder. Those large, deep, inscrutable eyes were presently fixed upon mine, when instantly placing his hands upon my forehead his touch produced an indescribable serenity and calmness, a calmness not born of earth, but at once peaceful, delightful and heavenly.

My whole being was imbued with a joy unspeakable. All feelings of sorrow instantly vanished. Those lines and shadows which care and sorrow impress upon us were dispelled as a deep fog before a blazing sun. In the eyes of my heavenly visitor, for such he appeared to me, there was a sort of lofty pity and tenderness infinitely stronger than any such feeling I ever saw manifested in ordinary mortals. His very calm appeared like a vast ocean stillness, at once overpowering to every agitated emotion.

By some intuition, or instinct, I felt he had something to communicate to soothe my sorrows and allay my apprehensions. Whereon, addressing me, he said:

"Son, I perceive thou hast grave anxieties over the perilous state of thy country, that thy soul has felt deep sorrow for its future. I have therefore come to thy relief and to tell thee of the causes that have led to this peril. Hear me attentively. Seventy-one years ago, after an awful apostasy of centuries, in which all nations were shrouded in spiritual darkness, when the angels had withdrawn themselves, the voice of the prophets hushed, and the light of Urim and Thummim shone not, and the vision of the seers was closed, while heaven itself shed not a ray of gladness to lighten a dark world, when Babel ruled and Satan laughed, and church and priesthood had taken their upward flight, and the voice of nations, possessing the books of the Jewish prophets, had ruled against vision and against Urim, against the further visits of angels, and against the doctrine of a church of apostles and prophets, thou knowest that then appeared a mighty angel with the solemn announcement of the hour of judgment, the burden of whose instructions pointed to dire calamities upon the present generation. This, therefore, is the cause of what thou seest and the end of the wicked hasteneth."

My vision now became extended in a marvelous manner, and the import of the past labors of the Elders was made plain to me. I saw multitudes fleeing to the place of safety in our mountain heights. The church was established in the wilderness. Simultaneously the nation had reached an unparalleled prosperity, wealth abounded, new territory was acquired, commerce extended, finance strengthened, confidence was maintained, and peoples abroad pointed to her as the model nation, the ideal of the past realized and perfected, the embodiment of the liberty sung by poets, and sought for by sages.

"But," continued the messenger, "Thou beholdest a change. Confidence is lost. Wealth is arrayed against labor, labor against wealth, yet the land abounds with plenty for food and raiment, and silver and gold are in abundance. Thou seest also that letters written by a Jew have wrought great confusion in the finances of the nation which, together with the policy of many wealthy ones, has produced distress and do presage further sorrow."

Factions now sprang up as if by magic; capital had entrenched itself against labor throughout the land; labor was organized against capital. The voice of the wise sought to tranquilize these two powerful factors in vain. Excited multitudes ran wildly about; strikes increased; lawlessness sought the place of regular government. At this juncture I saw a banner floating in air whereon was written the words Bankruptcy, Famine, Floods, Fire, Cyclones, Blood, Plague. Mad with rage men and women rushed upon each other. Blood flowed down the streets of cities like water. The demon of bloody hate had enthroned itself on the citadel of reason; the thirst for blood was intenser than that of the parched tongue for water. Thousands of bodies lay untombed in the streets.

Men and women fell dead from the terror inspired by fear. Rest was but the precursor of the bloody work of the morrow. All around lay the mournfulness of a past in ruins. Monuments erected to perpetuate the names of the noble and brave were ruthlessly destroyed by combustibles. A voice now sounded aloud these words, "Yet once again I shake not the earth only, but also heaven. And this word yet once again signifies the removing of things that are shaken, as of things that are made; that those things that cannot be shaken may remain."

Earthquakes rent the earth in vast chasms, which engulfed multitudes; terrible groanings and wailings filled the air; the shrieks of the suffering were indescribably awful. Water wildly rushed in from the tumultuous ocean whose very roaring under the mad rage of the fierce cyclone, was unendurable to the ear. Cities were swept away in an instant, missiles were hurled through the atmosphere at a terrible velocity and people were carried upward only to descend an unrecognized mass. Islands appeared where ocean waves once tossed the gigantic steamer. In other parts voluminous flames, emanating from vast fires, rolled with fearful velocity destroying life and property in their destructive course. The seal of the dread menace of despair was stamped on every human visage; men fell exhausted, appalled and trembling. Every element of agitated nature seemed a demon of wrathful fury. Dense clouds, blacker than midnight darkness, whose thunders reverberated with intonations which shook the earth, obscured the sunlight. Darkness reigned, unrivalled and supreme.

Again the light shone, revealing an atmosphere tinged with a leaden hue, which was the precursor of an unparalleled plague whose first symptoms were recognized by a purple spot which appeared on the cheek, or on the back of the hand, and which, invariably, enlarged until it spread over the entire surface of the body, producing certain death. Mothers, on sight of it, cast away their children as if they were poisonous reptiles.

This plague, in grown persons, rotted the eyes in their sockets and consumed the tongue as would a powerful acid or an intense heat. Wicked men, suffering under its writhing agonies, cursed God and died, as they stood on their feet, and the birds of prey feasted on their carcasses.

I saw in my dream the messenger again appear with a vial in his right hand, who addressing me said: "Thou knowest somewhat of the chemistry taught in the schools of human learning, behold now a chemistry sufficiently powerful to change the waters of the sea."

He then poured out his vial upon the sea and it became putrid as the blood of a dead man, and every living soul therein died. Other plagues followed I forbear to record.

A foreign power had invaded the nation which, from every human indication, it appeared would seize the government and supplant it with monarchy. I stood trembling at the aspect, when, lo, a power arose in the west which declared itself in favor of the constitution in its original form; to this suddenly rising power every lover of constitutional rights and liberties throughout the nation gave hearty support. The struggle was fiercely contested, but the stars and stripes floated in the breeze, and, bidding defiance to all opposition, waved proudly over the land. Among the many banners I saw, was one inscribed thus: "The government based on the Constitution, now and forever;" on another "Liberty of Conscience, social, religious, and political."

The light of the gospel which had but dimly shone because of abomination, now burst forth with a lustre that filled the earth. Cities appeared in every direction, one of which, in the centre of the continent, was an embodiment of architectural science after the pattern of eternal perfections, whose towers glittered with a radiance emanating from the sparkling of emeralds, rubies, diamonds and other precious stones set in a canopy of gold and so elaborately and skillfully arranged as to shed forth a brilliancy which dazzled and enchanted the eye, excited admiration and developed a taste for the beautiful, beyond anything man had ever conceived.

Fountains of crystal water shot upward their transparent jets which in the brilliant sunshine, formed ten thousand rainbow tints at once delightful to the eye. Gardens, the perfections of whose arrangement confound all our present attempts at genius, were bedecked with flowers of varied hue to develop and refine the taste, and strengthen a love for these nature's chastest adornments. Schools and universities were erected, to which all had access; in the latter Urims were placed, for the study of the past, present and future, and for obtaining a knowledge of the heavenly bodies, and of the constructions of worlds and universes.

The inherent properties of matter, its arrangements, laws, mutual relations were revealed and taught and made plain as the primer lesson of a child. The conflicting theories of geologists regarding the formation and age of the earth were settled forever. All learning was based on eternal certainty. Angels brought forth the treasures of knowledge which had lain hid in the womb of the dumb and distant past.

The appliances for making learning easily surpass all conjecture. Chemistry was rendered extremely simple, by the power which the Urims conferred on man of looking into and through the elements of every kind; a stone furnished no more obstruction to human vision than the air itself. Not only were the elements and all their changes and transformations plainly understood but the construction, operations, and laws of mind were thus rendered equally plain as those which governed the coarser elements.

While looking through the Urim and Thummim I was amazed at a transformation, which even now is to me marvellous beyond description, clearly showing the manner in which particles composing the inorganic kingdom of nature are conducted upward to become a part of organic forms; another astounding revelation was a view clearly shown me of the entire circulation of the blood both in man and animals. After seeing these things and gazing once more upon the beautiful city, the following passage of Scripture sounded in my ears: "Out of Zion the perfection of beauty God shineth."

On this I awoke to find all a dream.

I have written the foregoing, which is founded on true principle, under the caption of a dream, partly to instruct and partly to check the folly of reading silly novels now so prevalent.

Charles D. Evans
Springville, Utah

ABOUT THE AUTHOR

Hector Sosa Jr. was born in Puerto Rico. His family joined the LDS Church there when he was 13 years old, and they settled in southern Utah in 1982.

He served a mission for the Church in Barcelona, Spain.

He is currently a database engineer, and has worked with computers for more than two decades. He also runs several websites and four web forums.

He and his wife Tammy currently reside in Springville, Utah, and they are the parents of seven children.

Hector can be contacted at:

public-relations@springcreekbooks.com